To AUDREY.
FROM WINNIE.

CONTENTS

(FRONT COVER) *A sandstone window frames the trademark monoliths of Monument Valley.*
DAVID MUENCH
(INSIDE COVERS) *Trading post owner Lorenzo Hubbell encouraged Navajo rug weavers to make their work more saleable by incorporating red wool. This vibrant storm pattern is by Sarah Begay.*
JERRY JACKA

INTRODUCTION

Travel northeast out of Flagstaff and you enter Indian Country. Sprawling beyond the Utah border on the north and into New Mexico on the east — encompassing more than 16 million acres — these are the provinces of the Navajo and Hopi people. On the official *Arizona Travel Map*, Navajo and Hopi lands cover a vast dune-colored portion of the northeast quadrant of the state, scored off on the west by U.S. 89 and on the south by Interstate 40. You can drive north out of Flagstaff for more than 150 miles on U.S. 89 or east almost 200 miles on I-40, and the vast tablelands, elongated mesas, and knobby buttes of Indian Country still reach to the northern and eastern horizons.

Some roads traversing these lands are sketched on maps as bold red or black lines. These are the well-travelled, paved routes that take you to Tuba City, Chinle, Keams Canyon, Ganado, and Window Rock — historically important sites where in the past trading posts were established or where today federal offices or tribal governments are located.

Other roads are shown as crosshatch, or as skinny parallel lines. About these roads map legends warn, "Inquire locally." Sometimes maintained, sometimes not, in hard weather they often become running streams or hub-deep quagmires.

Many smaller roads, hundreds of them, are hidden from maps. You come upon them by surprise, side tracks, often deep-rutted, angling off main

(LEFT) *The Navajo Tribal Fair at Window Rock is held during the first week of September. Tribal members compete in two-step, skip dances, and singing.*
MONTY ROESSEL

roads, winding back across stark hills and disappearing over the horizon to no discernible destination.

It is unwise to try them. They are mostly unnavigable, except by local residents for whom these byways have become as familiar as the veins on the backs of their hands. These roads are an invitation to a busted axle, many miles from help. At the ends of these roads people still observe the old ways, sometimes speaking only their native language and living in dwellings made from native materials. Outsiders seldom see them — and, truth be told, local people prefer it that way.

◆   ◆   ◆   ◆   ◆

It is early August, the rainy season, and in late afternoon I'm driving west on U.S. 160 toward Tuba City, hoping to make Flagstaff, my home away from home, by nightfall. Earlier, around noon, hiking out of Tsegi Canyon after a two-day trek into the great Anasazi Pueblo Ruin, Keet Seel, I'd seen huge anvil-shaped thunderheads billowing above sheer canyon walls. At midday the sun was hot in the canyon bottom, and I welcomed the prospect of cooling rain. Not so welcome, though, were the loud thunderclaps accompanied by sudden darts of lightning. Twice, hiking out, I'd been forced to take cover.

Now, driving across the broad steppes of the Colorado Plateau, a place of endless sky, I can see dark rainy tendrils angling down from lowering cumulus clouds. But in the crackling dry atmosphere, they're yanked back to evaporate before they can pelt the parched earth. *Virgas*, these tendrils are called, Latin for twigs or whisks. The Navajo call it "ghost rain," or the "hair of the rain."

This is Great Basin desert scrub, dry country, where even during monsoon season very little rain actually falls to the ground — sometimes only an inch or two annually. Most of the precipitation arrives as snow, often heavy, during cold winters.

The land wears a thin skin on these plains, rubbed raw by slashing rain, scorching sun, and winds that sometimes approach hurricane velocity. Sagebrush, saltbush, winterfat, bunch grasses, and a few other plants grow at roadside. Hardy in winter, adapted to prolonged drought in summer, they thrive here. In the wetter uplands, atop long mesas, there are mixed pines, oaks, piñon, juniper, mountain mahogany, and cliffrose. And in the cooler, still wetter microclimates of some of the deeper canyons are Douglas fir and quaking aspen.

The remarkably varied physiography of Indian Country encompasses barren, eroded hills; slumped cliffs and cones; and rain-severed gullies of the Painted Desert. It also includes the wind-sculpted buttes of Monument Valley, the pine forest atop Navajo Mountain, the watery immensity of Lake Powell, the lava-capped summits of the Hopi Mesas, and the enchanted Petrified Forest.

As I turn south on U.S. 89 toward Flagstaff, sporadic raindrops splatter my windshield. I wonder if I'll see water flowing under the bridge near Cameron where the highway crosses the Little Colorado. So far the rain here has been too light to swell the river with runoff, but heavy downpours out of sight upstream can bring flash flooding in a matter of seconds and turn otherwise dry riverbeds into raging torrents.

Only a trickle of water flows in the Little Colorado when I cross, but beyond Cameron the sky is heavily overcast. Although I cannot see them, I'm climbing toward the San Francisco Peaks and Flagstaff. In clear weather the peaks — the dwelling place of spirits important in the mythologies of Hopi, Navajo, and other Indian people — would be visible by now. As my truck climbs, the rain builds to a steady patter on the cab.

Cooler air seeps in through the vents as I head toward Flagstaff's 7,000-foot elevation. I

(ABOVE) *Navajo Sarah Whitehorse tends her flock.* JERRY JACKA
(RIGHT) *Sculpted by centuries of erosion, Monument Valley spires punctuate the skyline.* MICHAEL COLLIER

switch on the heater, feeling a little silly about it in midsummer. Lulled into reverie by the steady rhythm of the windshield wipers, I begin to think of my cabin in the woods just outside town. I'll build a warm fire and rest for a day or two, sorting through my gear, studying maps, plotting an itinerary of my continuing odyssey through Indian Lands.

◆　◆　◆　◆　◆

A plan begins to take shape in my mind. I will use Flagstaff as my base for excursions into Indian Country. Moving along lines radiating from this hub, I can approach destinations near and far. Some will be day trips, starting and ending in Flagstaff.

Ranging out clockwise from Flagstaff are more far-flung destinations. My plan divides the territory into rough fourths and groups destinations within each. So, after Flagstaff my first group of destinations is the Page-Tuba City area. Points of interest include Glen Canyon Dam, Lake Powell, and Rainbow Bridge; Lees Ferry, and Glen Canyon; Antelope Canyon and other slot canyons; Betatakin and Keet Seel Ruins at Navajo National Monument; and one or more dinosaur-track locations.

From Page-Tuba City I can travel east toward historic Gouldings Lodge and Trading Post in the heart of Monument Valley. Then I can drive to the historic marker at Four Corners before heading south to Canyon de Chelly National Monument, then on to the Hubbell Trading Post at Ganado and east to the Navajo Nation capital at Window Rock.

My final group of destinations starts at Meteor Crater and proceeds east on I-40 to Petrified Forest National Park and portions of the Painted Desert lying within the park. The Hopi Indian Reservation and the villages of Walpi, Oraibi, Hotevilla, and Shongopovi on the Hopi mesas are also among the places grouped within the final area on my itinerary. At the Hopi Villages perhaps I will be able to witness some of the ceremonial dances.

Along the way, there are other destinations. Many times in my travels across Indian Country I've passed small trading posts but had no time to visit. On this trip I'll stop. Homolovi Ruins State Park, one of Arizona's newest and a place I have not yet visited, is also on my mental list.

Finally, because natural history was important to the lives of the early people who settled here and is vital to knowing how these places became what they are, I resolve to keep careful notes on the geology, weather, flora, and fauna.

◆　◆　◆　◆　◆

I enter Flagstaff in a driving rain, run into a quick-shop place for breakfast fixings, and make straight for my cabin in the woods. Tonight, it'll feel good to sit by the fire sipping a hot drink. But thinking about the territory ahead has rekindled my appetite for travel. I'm eager to restock my outfit, as oldtimers used to say, and get back on the road.

Tom Dollar

Tom Dollar

A regular contributor to Arizona Highways *magazine, Tom Dollar has also written for* The New York Times, Audubon, Omni, Discover, The Mother Earth News, *and many other national publications. This is his first book for* Arizona Highways.

(ABOVE) *A hiker studies well-preserved dinosaur prints in the Glen Canyon Recreation Area.*
GARY LADD
(OPPOSITE PAGE) *With the snow-covered San Francisco Peaks in the distance, the walls of Lomaki Ruin at Wupatki National Monument are illuminated by a morning sun.*
DAVID MUENCH

Chapter 1 ◆ Indian Country

FLAGSTAFF AREA

Museum of Northern Arizona

The place to start exploring Indian Country is the Museum of Northern Arizona, located just 3 miles northwest of downtown Flagstaff along Fort Valley Road (U.S. 180), the highway to the Grand Canyon. Now more than 60 years old, the museum is committed to interpreting and preserving the natural and cultural history of the Colorado Plateau, a geological province that includes parts of Arizona, Utah, Colorado, and New Mexico.

"Splendid, stunning, overwhelming" spring to mind when describing the Museum of Northern Arizona's collections. But even these superlatives understate the extent of the museum's holdings in archaeology, ethnology, geology, biology, and the fine arts. The number of artifacts contained in its archaeological and ethnographic collections alone totals more than one million.

The museum is best experienced in small doses over time. On one visit I spent an entire afternoon looking at samples of Indian weaving. It was almost too much for the senses. Weeks earlier, I had whiled away a morning studying some of the more than 20,000 fossil, rock, and mineral specimens.

As if its permanent collections were not enough, the Museum of Northern Arizona displays several changing exhibits each year. During one recent season visitors were treated to "Dinosaurs: A

(LEFT) *After their arrival in the area some 1,400 years ago, the Sinagua built these 800-year-old cliff dwellings.*
CHUCK PLACE

Global View," a travelling exhibit previously featured at such prestigious institutions as the Royal Ontario Museum and the American Museum of Natural History.

Other exhibits, such as the Hopi, Navajo, and Zuni artists exhibitions, are scheduled annually. The museum craft shop offers one of the finest selections of traditional and contemporary Indian pottery, weaving, basketry, carving, and jewelry to be found anywhere. I urge travelers in Indian Country to become familiar with Navajo, Hopi, and Zuni arts and crafts by making their first stop the Museum of Northern Arizona in Flagstaff.

Walnut Canyon National Monument

It's mid-morning. I'm standing on a narrow walkway almost 200 feet below the rim of Walnut Canyon. The walkway encircles a lava-capped limestone obelisk rising from the middle of Walnut Creek. Formed millions of years ago when an earthquake blocked Walnut Creek's main channel, forcing water to cut another route, this large stone pinnacle is called Third Fort Island. From the walkway, I'm peering into a small room nestled into the hollow of a shallow cave.

The pale beam of my pocket flashlight probes the corners of the tiny room. The walls, constructed of irregular limestone blocks and thick mud mortar, are soot-stained from decades of cooking fires. The entrance is T-shaped, a design intended to serve as both door and chimney, with smoke escaping the room near the lintel.

Inside, small openings on opposite sides of the room, appearing scarcely big enough for a child to squeeze through, lead to adjacent rooms. These tiny cliff-perched apartments are repeated many times throughout the canyon — rooms for cooking and sleeping, others for storage, and a larger common room erected like a capstone atop the pinnacle for trade or ceremonials. Outside the single entrance is a narrow ledge, widened somewhat and paved for tourists like me, with a dizzying 200-foot plummet to the canyon floor below.

I try to imagine life in these tiny rooms with their very low ceilings. Meager furnishings — woven mats for sitting on the floor, a metate for grinding corn, cooking pots, a few tools — would not have used much space. But even allowing for the fact that the people who called these small cells home were much shorter than my six feet, it would have been cramped. Damp and cold, too, or when heated with juniper and piñon fires, smoke-choked. Except at night or times when they sought shelter from bad weather, these cliff dwellers lived outdoors.

(ABOVE) *In summer the Bonito Park area of Coconino National Forest becomes a sea of sunflower yellow.*
JACK DYKINGA
(RIGHT) *Dancers make their grand entrance during the annual Indian Days Pow Wow in downtown Flagstaff.*
TOM BEAN

Who were the Pueblo Indians who lived here intermittently for about 150 years? How did they live? What was the quality of daily life in Walnut Canyon? Why did they leave? Where did they go?

Archaeologists call them Sinagua, a name borrowed from an early Spanish designation for the San Francisco mountains, Sierra Sin Agua, meaning "mountains without water." The Sinagua can be traced back to the year A.D. 600 when they apparently came from the region of what is now southeastern Arizona to this arid country east of the San Francisco Peaks.

Despite the scarcity of water, life in Walnut Canyon thrived. Like today's Hopi Indians, the Sinagua were dry-land farmers, cultivating corn, beans, and several varieties of squash in extensive rim-top fields and washes. These farmers were expert water and soil conservationists. In the canyon bottom they constructed check dams, which slowed the flow of water, soaked up winter snow, and collected nutrient-rich topsoils.

I wish I were as sure-footed as the Sinagua must have been. Then I could trace one of the pathways worn along natural erosion lines in the canyon walls to the drainage bottom. Via these paths, cliff dwellers descended from their homes to work small creek-side garden plots and to carry water from deep pools in the creek bed.

The growing season at elevations approaching 7,000 feet is short. Because Walnut Creek did not flow year-round, the Sinagua had to rely completely on snow melt and rainwater for their crops. Farming in Walnut Canyon was difficult. Still, the Sinagua were successful enough in most years to store food, and they apparently traded surplus foods to other Indians.

No one is certain why the Sinagua abandoned their cliff dwellings in Walnut Canyon. No evidence supports the conclusion that they were driven out by rival groups. But it is possible that their farming methods wore out the soils, that they picked the area clean by intensive foraging, that

GRAND FALLS

DON STEVENSON

Lowering clouds spit occasional darts of icy rain on the cold, raw day in early March when I first stood above Grand Falls on the Little Colorado River. Tons of silty water tumbled over the cataract into a ginger-colored maelstrom below me, throwing off a fine mist that swirled against my face. Watching all that sepia water surge past, I thought, "Well there goes the Painted Desert," recalling the many washes branching like tree limbs across the Painted Desert that drain into the Little Colorado and are funneled here to plunge 185 feet into what

the Hopi Indians call the "swishing-whistling-sound place."

Grand Falls was formed about a thousand years ago when lava from the volcanic eruption of Merriam Crater, some 10 miles west of the Little Colorado, dammed its channel. Forced to detour around the dam, the river filled to the level of the surrounding plateau and poured back into the gorge over the rim of its own canyon, creating a cascade 18 feet higher than Niagara Falls. Slowed to a trickle or dry most of the year, the Little Colorado becomes a swollen torrent during spring snow melt or periods of violent summer thunderstorms. When that happens, Grand Falls lives up to its name.

Getting there: After driving about 8 miles east from Flagstaff on the Camp Townsend-Winona Road, turn left onto the Leupp Road. Travel approximately 15 miles to a sign that announces "Grand Falls Bible Church, 1 mile." Turn left onto Navajo Route 70. Nine miles of gravel-to-dirt-road driving will bring you to Grand Falls.

Caution: While people with sedans may make the trip, high-clearance vehicles are best suited for this road. In wet weather portions of this road may be impassable even for four-wheel-drive vehicles.

they killed most of the small game upon which they were very dependent, and that they were forced to travel great distances to forage for edible wild foods, meat, and firewood for cooking and warmth. Perhaps all of these reasons, combined with 30 years of prolonged drought, prompted a gradual withdrawal to other areas.

Where did they go? The most logical explanation is that they merged with other Indian groups. Today, some Hopi clans revere Walnut Canyon as their ancestral home, and archaeological findings support the link.

In late afternoon I watch shadows drop into the canyon and lengthen steadily. I've been sitting with my back to a rock on the south face of Third Fort Island. But soon even that comfortable perch is blanketed in gray light. The temperature drops. Reluctantly, I rise to hike toward bright sunlight still showing on the rim.

As I turn to leave, I think, "Just now would be the hour when a Sinagua farmer, after tilling his fields all day on the rim, would trudge homeward into the canyon." Climbing, I glance up now and then, half expecting to meet someone.

A hush falls over the landscape as evening descends, and I slow my pace, reluctant to leave. "I would live here," I say to myself. "For a while it must have been paradise."

◆　◆　◆　◆　◆

Sunset Crater Volcano & Wupatki National Monument

Ravens and snow-capped peaks. Certain images stick in the mind. On the road that loops through Sunset Crater Volcano and Wupatki national monuments to connect with U.S. 89, ravens are everywhere. They cruise the flat lands and cavort in pairs and triplets above mesas and cinder cones. Unlike the smaller, warier crows, they readily deviate from straight-line flight, peeling off toward anything that stimulates their curiosity, including me. As I hike the lava fields or tour the Wupatki, Lomaki, and Wukoki ruins, they cruise past on strong wings to check me out.

The peaks are the volcanic San Francisco Mountains — Doyle, Humphreys, Agassiz, and Fremont peaks. At 12,643 feet, Humphreys Peak, the heart of the 19,000-acre Kachina Peaks

(RIGHT) Colorful rabbitbush and aspen trees provide sharp contrast to the stark cinder cones of Sunset Crater.
TOM DANIELSEN

Wilderness, is the highest in Arizona. Wherever I go, the peaks loom in the near distance. Whether walking the hardened magma of the Bonito Lava flows, circling the base of rust-hued spatter cones, or puzzling over the large amphitheater and ball court at the Wupatki Ruin, when I look up, the peaks are there — in mid-spring still snowcapped above timberline.

The claim of the Navajo and Hopi on these mountains is much older than ours. The names they gave to the peaks honor the powers of the spirit world, not the accomplishments of mortals. These mountains were sacred to native people going back generations before the Navajo and Hopi. I try to imagine the reverence of those who went out to work in the fields or sat before a doorway grinding corn in a place where their most hallowed of shrines was so constant a presence.

The San Francisco Peaks stand at the center of a vast 2,200-square-mile volcanic field in the southwest corner of the Colorado Plateau. Nine-hundred-dred-year-old Sunset Crater is the youngest volcano in Arizona, coming at the end of a period of volcanism that had already lasted for several million years before the crater's eruption. It must have been an unearthly time, during the winter of A.D. 1064-65, when a relatively tiny fissure in the Earth's crust

began to hiss steam and belch fiery cinders into the atmosphere.

More than 400 volcanoes and hundreds of mini-volcanoes, known as fumaroles and spatter cones, were already active. The earth trembled, hot gases seethed from cracks and vents, and clouds of ash swirled in the air. The Sinagua, who farmed here, may have escaped in time to save themselves from the volcano's devasta-

tion. In the 1930s, excavations of pit houses revealed that those who fled Sunset Crater's explosion removed not only their belongings but also the building timbers from their homes. Clearly, they intended to relocate and rebuild elsewhere.

Other timbers found in some of the more than 800 ruins within the monument and in the Wupatki Pueblo itself helped date the eruption of Sunset

Crater. When archaeologists examined the growth rings of these timbers, they found that a period of severe stunting occurred in A.D. 1064 or 1065. From this evidence investigators surmised that trees that produced these timbers survived the volcanic eruption but were badly damaged by intense heat, flying cinders, and clouds of ash.

Sunset Crater's eruption reached its peak sometime between A.D. 1065 and 1090. Lava flowed from the base of the volcano in 1150 and again in 1220. The last burst from the cone itself, which produced the red cinders that settled around the rim and gave the crater its name, came in 1250. Although Sunset Crater and other volcanoes in this area are now extinct, the field itself is potentially active. In 1983, in fact, the U.S. Geological Survey included the San Francisco Volcanic Field in a list of 35 volcanoes in the western United States, Hawaii, and Alaska that were likely to erupt again.

Prior to Sunset Crater's eruption, a very small population had managed a hardscrabble subsistence farming on land in the vicinity. Ironically, although it uprooted some people, the volcanic explosion produced a cultural explosion as well. The volcano laid waste to everything near its epicenter, scorching the vegetation and smothering the land beneath layers of lava or ash. Survivors moved just beyond the volcano's circle of devastation and resettled.

Away from the cone a light covering of ash and cinders helped the soil absorb and hold moisture. Plants thrived. Soon, farmers of diverse cultures began to move back, and this fertile, now well-watered agricultural zone became a melting pot. Immigrants arriving from the south brought Hohokam traditions; those from the north imported Anasazi ways. The 100-room, three-story Wupatki (Hopi for Rain Cloud) pueblo, with its Hohokam-style ball court and Anasazi-inspired Great Kiva, shows the completeness of this acculturation.

Tree-ring dating indicates that this promising civilization was cut short by a drought that began in A.D. 1150 and lasted for an estimated 30 years. By A.D. 1170, many of Wupatki's inhabitants began leaving the area in search of more hospitable homesteads. Most moved south to the Verde Valley or to the northeast where they lived with the Hopi. Archaeologists conclude this once-thriving cultural center was abandoned by the year 1225 because of drought and other factors.

Today, only the ravens and other wild denizens seem able to survive in this bleak, forsaken land. Whether sublime silhouettes soaring against the backdrop of snow-shrouded peaks or common vagabonds rooting in tourist trash barrels, the ravens have staked their claim.

◆ **Museum of Northern Arizona**
Route 4, Box 720
Flagstaff, AZ 86001
602-774-5211

◆ **Sunset Crater Volcano National Monument**
Route 3, Box 149
Flagstaff, AZ 86004
602-556-7042

◆ **Walnut Canyon National Monument**
Walnut Canyon Road
Flagstaff, AZ 86004
602-526-3367

◆ **Wupatki National Monument**
HC 33, Box 444A
Flagstaff, AZ 86004
602-556-7040

(TOP, LEFT) *This turn-of-the-century Hemis Kachina doll (Home Dancer) stands 15 inches tall.*
JERRY JACKA
(ABOVE) *Wupatki National Monument encompasses more than 800 rock dwellings.*
DICK DIETRICH
(LEFT) *Wukoki Ruin, framed by junipers, is bathed in early morning light.*
JACK DYKINGA

Chapter 2 ◆ Indian Country

LAKE POWELL & NAVAJO NATIONAL MONUMENT

Glen Canyon

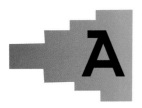**A** party of raft passengers stands on the beach before a soaring petroglyph mural in Glen Canyon a few miles below the dam. We're a polyglot group. There are the Swiss honeymooners, the retired couple from France, the businessman and his wife from Milan, and the Germans. The dialects of English spoken here must have the Europeans wondering how many flavors there are in one language. There's the jeweler from New York city, the machinist from Boston, and the farmer from Alabama. To spice the potpourri there's an Australian geologist.

The Frenchman, in heavily accented English, asks the "edge" of the figures pecked into the dark stains on the wall. Our young boatman and guide seems perplexed.

"He wants to know their 'age,'" I say, helpfully.

"Oh, I get it," he says with a laugh, then explains that they were put here by the prehistoric Anasazi Indians who dwelled in Glen Canyon for almost 1,000 years until about A.D. 1250.

The mural, yards long, suggests a history of daily life told in pictures. The walls are a visual feast of clan symbols, sun signs, mazes, and squiggly lines. One long line, our guide points out, is a fairly accurate representation of the Colorado River channel as it runs through this section of Glen Canyon.

(LEFT) *Now a staging area for raft trips down the Colorado River, Lees Ferry was once the only crossing for hundreds of miles upstream or downstream.*
DAVID MUENCH

Animal figures abound too. There are bighorn sheep, pronghorns, and birds. Low on the wall, a raptor, perhaps a peregrine falcon, stoops upon something concealed beneath the sand. At one time other pictures were visible here, but loads of sand deposited by the river's surge have buried them. The falcon's prey may forever remain a mystery.

◆　　◆　　◆　　◆　　◆

Just after dawn we had boarded a bus in Page for our ride to the base of Glen Canyon Dam. Rafts operated by Wilderness River Adventures waited to float us downstream through a 16-mile relic of Glen Canyon, the remnant of a vast canyon that once stretched for miles along the four-corners border from the mouth of the Paria River to the mouth of the San Juan. Alternately drifting and motoring, our destination is Lees Ferry where John D. Lee ferried passengers across the Colorado in the 19th century. Until the construction in 1929 of the steel bridge at Marble Canyon, 6 miles downstream, the ferry was the only way across. Today Lees Ferry is the staging area for Colorado River trips through the Grand Canyon.

Only photographs show its former splendor but, judging from what we're seeing this morning, Glen Canyon was a place of surpassing beauty. The steep walls, streaked by manganese-oxide stains that create the effect of dark tapestry, rise hundreds of feet above the river. The trill of canyon wrens cascades from the heights. Ospreys and ravens soar, coming to perch in niches out of sight high on the cliff face. Mallards scoot in pairs along the shoreline.

By mid-morning the sun finds the river bottom to burn off the chill, and we strip to t-shirts and shorts. Floating with the current, we pass motorboats carrying fishermen upstream. The water released from the bottom of the dam is a frigid 45 degrees. That is too cold for swimming, unless you're a rainbow trout. From time to time we catch sight of a lunker trout holding against the current.

When we reach Lees Ferry we have time for a quick tour of the cabin at "Lonely Dell," John Lee's name for his homestead. Several crews are rigging big rafts for trips through the Grand Canyon. Passengers waiting on shore for the adventure of a lifetime assemble personal gear, packing it into watertight rubber bags and surplus ammo cans. We watch the show enviously until our bus driver summons us aboard for the return trip to Page.

(TOP) *Glen Canyon Dam rises 710 feet above the river.*
(ABOVE) *A 16-mile raft trip below the dam to Lees Ferry tours the only stretch of Glen Canyon not filled by Lake Powell.*
(RIGHT) *These petroglyphs are the work of the Anasazi, who lived here more than 750 years ago.*
ALL BY ROBERT J. FARRELL

LONELY DELL

Jacob Hamblin, one of the great trailblazers of the West, located this site on the banks of the Colorado River in the 1860s. In 1872 Brigham Young, president of the Mormon church, assigned John D. Lee to establish a ferry service to assist migrating settlers.

Early in December of that year, Lee, his 14-year-old son, and two men drove 57 head of cattle out of southern Utah through the Paria River gorge towards the Grand Canyon. Fifty miles and eight days later, having battled cold weather, icy waters, and quicksand that swallowed up cows, the Lee party arrived at the river. Only 12 head of cattle survived.

Christmas was celebrated in a temporary shelter, but by mid-January two houses had been built. Later, Lee brought two of his 18 wives to settle the Lees Ferry area. When one of them, Emma, first saw the site, she exclaimed, "Oh, what a lonely dell!" The name stuck.

Lee, however, was a fugitive from justice. He was wanted by federal authorities for his part in the 1857 Mountain Meadows Massacre in which an immigrant party was slaughtered by farmers and Indians. Continually on the run from federal marshals, Lee was absent most of the time, so Emma operated the ferry. Lee was arrested in 1874 and, after two trials, was convicted. He was killed by a firing squad on March 23, 1877.

This was the only crossing of the Colorado for hundreds of miles upstream or downstream. Thousands of wagons and early automobiles used the crude ferry boats until 1929 when Navajo Bridge was completed.

Today, Lonely Dell is maintained by the National Park Service and consists of a root cellar, a log cabin, a blacksmith shop, buildings erected by those who followed Lee, and a cemetery located a quarter-mile up Paria Canyon. The original ferry site is located in the Lees Ferry Historic District near the present launch ramp and parking area.

A rock structure, built as a trading post to help maintain peace with the Navajo, is commonly called Lees Ferry Fort. Another rock building was used by the American Placer Company, a gold mining operation owned by Charles H. Spencer. The remains of the Charles H. Spencer, a 92-foot-long steamboat used by the mining company, can still be seen.

(**BELOW**) *Emma Lee ran the ferry her husband founded from her primitive log cabin (background) at Lonely Dell.*
JACK DYKINGA

◆ ◆ ◆ ◆ ◆

Lake Powell

In 1963 the last of 10 million buckets of concrete was poured and Glen Canyon Dam was finished. Slowly, water backed up behind the dam, and the canyon that John Wesley Powell explored and named for the beauty of its "many glens or coves" began to disappear. It took seven years to build the dam and seventeen years to fill the lake. By 1980, when Lake Powell reached "full pool," more than 26 million acre feet of water had been impounded.

The dam created a monster lake with a shoreline of 1,960 miles, longer than the entire east coast of the United States. Exploring its channels, bays, and myriad canyons could take a lifetime.

Like any large body of water, the nearly 200-mile-long Lake Powell changes moods quickly. A few years ago on a week-long sea kayak trip, I learned something about Powell's unpredictable temperament. We had camped for the night near the mouth of Gunsight Canyon. The evening was balmy, the bay beside us mirror smooth. Past midnight I awoke to the sound of a freshening breeze. Smiling at the prospect of cooler weather, I rolled over in my bedroll and went back to sleep.

Just after sunrise we launched our two small double-seater kayaks for the long paddle back to Wahweap Marina where we had launched five days ago. As we sailed out of the protected bay onto the

(ABOVE) *In addition to 96 major canyons, Lake Powell has hundreds of narrow passageways, some just wide enough for kayakers to navigate.*
JACK DYKINGA
(RIGHT) *The fiery hues of buttes near Padre Bay are accentuated by the setting sun.*
GARY LADD

lake, we were sideswiped by a strong westerly breeze that put a serious chop on the water. Quickly, we slipped into our flotation vests and fastened the watertight spray decks around the cockpits of our boats.

By mid-afternoon we were paddling in truly rough waters straight into a wind gusting to an estimated 35 knots. Whitecaps, cresting from two to four feet, bared their foamy teeth as they broke across our bows. Barely making one knot even with strenuous effort, our tiny boats, their decks constantly awash, must have appeared in great jeopardy. The pilot of a houseboat slowed and called to see if we needed help. We waved him off.

But as we rounded a point into even rougher waters, a strong gust slammed the bows of our boats, lifting them perilously out of the water. Quickly we maneuvered into a sheltered inlet on the lee side of the peninsula. The wind continued unabated. We decided to cook our supper where we sat and hoped that later the wind would die, allowing us to paddle under a full moon 2 miles to a campsite beneath Romana Mesa. That would place us, weather permitting, within an easy half-day's ride of the marina although we had provisioned our boats for two extra days just in case.

The wind did die down, we made it to Romana Mesa, and by noon the next day, having hauled our

boats ashore for the last time, we were breakfasting on steak and eggs at a cafe in Page.

For some, water recreation defines Lake Powell. Houseboating, powerboating, water skiing, jet skiing, sailing, canoeing, kayaking, fishing, and shore camping are among the water-related sports available. But onshore activities — hiking, backpacking, and exploring the back country canyons around the lake — are also popular.

For others, sightseeing is what it's all about. Eons of wind and water erosion have chiseled a fantastic geometry on the sandstone around Lake Powell. Cones, towers, buttes, mesas, minarets, cliffs, domes, bluffs, obelisks, turrets, amphitheaters, grot-

toes, steeples, fins — in infinite shades of gray, ocher, and mauve — are brought into stark relief by the sparseness of vegetation.

A year after our kayak trip, I toured parts of the lake aboard a powerboat piloted by Steve Ward, public relations director at Wahweap Lodge and Marina. Steve grew up in Page before the dam was built, and he watched the lake fill up. He knows Lake Powell as well as anyone.

In one day we covered more water than I had managed in a week aboard my kayak. At noon we sailed into Twilight Canyon where we dove from the boat's bow into a seemingly bottomless blue-green pool. After lunch we napped in the shade below a keyhole carved by wind and water into an immense sandstone obelisk streaked with the most impressive mineral-stained tapestry I'd seen.

Later we zipped up the lake to Forbidding Canyon, the site of Rainbow Bridge. Before Glen Canyon Dam was built, getting to Rainbow Bridge was an arduous back country trek. Now visitors arrive by boat and need take only a short hike.

We hiked up Aztec Canyon, a branch of Forbidding Canyon, to Echo Camp to find a little spring and the foundations of some old buildings. Many trees grew near the spring. The oasis was quiet and green. In the back of a water-scooped alcove above the spring was a rock ledge where, ages ago, people had retreated in summer to escape the heat. We too climbed to the ledge and enjoyed the soothing shade. At sunset, our bodies tired but our spirits refreshed, we cruised slowly back to the marina.

(OPPOSITE PAGE) *After piloting their motorized hotel to a secluded cove, houseboaters set up base camp before exploring their surroundings.*
DICK DIETRICH

(ABOVE, LEFT) *Wahweap Lodge and Marina, the principal recreational facility on Lake Powell, features hotel accommodations, a campground, picnic ramadas, restaurants, a swimming beach, and a boat-launch ramp.*
GARY LADD

(LEFT) *With all of its side canyons, the 186-mile-long lake has more shoreline than the east coast of the U.S., allowing you to choose your own slice of paradise.*
RALPH LEE HOPKINS

(FOLLOWING PANEL) *The world's largest natural rock span, Rainbow Bridge is just north of the Arizona-Utah border. It is tall enough to fit the dome of the United States Capitol beneath it.*
DAVID MUENCH

Navajo National Monument: Betatakin

Although I'd seen photographs of it, Betatakin took me by surprise. You approach through a wooded canyon thick with Douglas fir, quaking aspen, and oak. It's moist here and cool, giving trees like aspen and fir, which usually grow only in high mountains, a canyon niche that feels like home. Suddenly, there it is. Tucked inside a vaulted sandstone alcove — 450 feet high, 370 feet wide, and 152 feet deep — is Betatakin, Navajo for "ledge house." The blend of sandstone masonry against a sandstone backdrop gives the 135-room structure a natural camouflage. Perhaps it also explains why archaeologist Byron Cummings did not "discover" Betatakin until 1909, 14 years after the discovery of Keet Seel, the largest of the ruins at Navajo National Monument.

It is early June, springtime in plateau country. Cliff rose, Fendlerbush, penstemon, larkspur, and wild rose bloom along the rim and beside the trail descending into Tsegi Canyon. The day is sunny and bright, the air calm, the temperature a perfect 70 degrees. Our guide talks about the layered sandstone, "petrified sand dunes" he calls them. He also explains that when water percolating through soft Navajo Sandstone hits the denser, impermeable Kayenta Formation, it is forced to run laterally, creating perennial springs at the bases of cliffs.

Amazingly, it is this slow trickle of water that actually carved out the caves in which the Anasazi built their masonry dwellings. Water — oozing, seeping, dripping — collected behind layers of sandstone and froze when temperatures dropped. The expanding ice caused sheets of sandstone to break off and crash to the rocks below where wind and rain furthered their erosion. This slow but inexorable spalling away of the cave walls continues still, resulting in several rooms at Betatakin being destroyed by rock falls.

It's easy to see why Anasazi farmers made their homes here. The deep alcove faces south, capturing the sun's warm rays in winter months. And with the sun tracking well north of the great overhang during summer, the rooms within the alcove stay shady and cool.

The springs provided a ready and dependable source of water. In fields a mile or so away the farmers grew corn, beans, and squash, a diet they supplemented with seeds, nuts, and berries in season. And of course they hunted rabbits, squirrels,

birds, and occasionally, deer, bighorn sheep, or pronghorn.

By the middle of the 13th century when Betatakin was built, the Kayenta Anasazi, as the anthropologists called them, were making beautiful polychrome pottery. Pot makers, weavers of fine baskets and textiles, excellent masons, skilled gardeners, and expert hunters, the Anasazi led a settled, integrated life here in Tsegi Canyon. Yet they abandoned Betatakin around A.D. 1300, having occupied it for less than a half century.

All that work, and then gone. The reasons are difficult to determine, although there is no evidence of warfare. Like other people throughout the Southwest, the Anasazi probably left Betatakin for a combination of reasons: erosion that carried off fertile topsoil, excessive woodcutting that depleted supplies for cooking, heating, and building, and 30 years of drought that dried up water sources. Unable to farm, the Anasazi deserted their homes, leaving behind an architectural masterpiece and haunting questions.

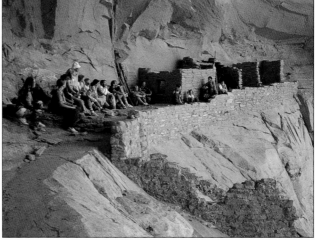

(TOP) *An estimated 20 to 25 families could not overcome challenges that caused them to abandon this cliff dwelling around* A.D. *1300.*
JERRY JACKA

(ABOVE) *During the summer, park rangers lead four-hour hiking tours to Betatakin.*
JAMES TALLON

(LEFT) *Anasazi cooking fires once carried the fragrance of corn, beans, and squash.* JERRY JACKA

◆ ◆ ◆ ◆ ◆

Keet Seel

So many ceramic artifacts were found at Tsegi Canyon's largest Anasazi ruin that the Navajo named it Keet Seel, "broken pottery." Tree-ring dating of roof beams and other timbers reveals that the Anasazi occupied Keet Seel as early as A.D. 950, about 300 years before Betatakin, and departed at about the same time as the withdrawal from other pueblos in the area.

Travel to Keet Seel is either by horseback or foot. I chose to walk. Twice. The first time, I hiked the 16-mile round trip from the Navajo National Monument Visitor Center in a single day. It was a strenuous all-day walk. Although a great hike, I spent too much time walking and not enough enjoying the scenery. The second time, I obtained a permit from the National Park Service to camp in an oak grove near the ruin and backpacked to Keet Seel.

Keet Seel deserves a long look, not only because of its impressive architecture and masonry construction, but also because of its setting. Centuries of rainwater washing from the canyon rim across the vaulted ceiling has stained it with iron- and manganese-oxide striations hundreds of feet long, creating an incredibly beautiful tapestry effect.

Led by a Park Service guide who lived in a small

(**ABOVE**) *The Anasazi used underground kivas, of which there are several at Keet Seel, for ceremonial purposes and as a sort of men's club for the different clans.*
GARY LADD
(**RIGHT**) *With 160 rooms, Keet Seel is the largest cliff dwelling in Arizona. Since only 25 people are allowed to make the trek to the monument each day, reservations are required.*
JEFF GNASS

cabin nearby, we climbed a ladder into the ruins and looked around. In late afternoon, shadows spread into the recess, blurring the outlines of roofs and corners. At sunset we watched from below as the granaries, kivas, and family dwellings faded into the twilight.

We timed our visit to coincide with the full moon and kept watch into the night as the moon crested the canyon rim to cast a ghostly pallor on the ruins. Rising in the early morning dark, we watched the great pueblo come into focus in the gray light of dawn and held our breaths as the sun slanted to illuminate the alcove. I felt like I was seeing Keet Seel for the first time.

◆ **Glen Canyon National Recreation Area**
P.O. Box 1507
Page, AZ 86040
602-645-8200

◆ **Lake Powell ARA Leisure Services**
P.O. Box 56909
Phoenix, AZ 85079
602-278-8888
800-528-6154

◆ **Navajo National Monument**
HC 71, Box 3
Tonalea, AZ 86044-9704
602-672-2366

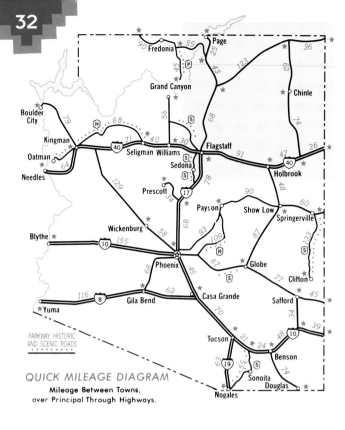

NORTHEASTERN ARIZONA

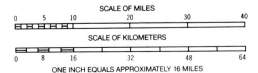

MONUMENT VALLEY & CANYON DE CHELLY NATIONAL MONUMENT

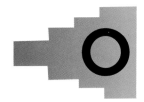

Monument Valley

Our guide is a Navajo named Kee. He is a storehouse of information but a man of few words. It's a relief from the usual tour-guide onslaught, a continual stream of chattering detail that you learn to tune out. I like the long silences between nuggets of information, punctuated only by the noise of the laboring engine as the big four-wheel-drive chugs through deep sand. Or when we've stopped, the hiss of sand grains as a breeze moves them across the dunes, the chattering of birds 300 feet up a cliff face, and the happy laughter of the two 12-year-old girls in our party as they scamper up boulder faces as nimbly as bighorn lambs.

Kee speaks. I snap to attention. "The small trees on the rim there are piñon," he says. "Some are more than 300 years old. They don't grow fast." A nugget. I write it down in my notebook. This isn't the kind of stuff you read in the guide books.

He brakes the truck beside a small bush, blooming white. "The bush with flowers is cliffrose," he explains. "Navajo people call it 'baby-diaper' plant. They used to put the soft bark in the cradle boards to keep the baby dry." As the day goes on, my notebook begins to fill with more nuggets of informa-

(LEFT) *Every major butte and spire in Monument Valley has been given a name. A small portion of Elephant Butte is in the foreground, while Rabbit and Stagecoach buttes are in the distance.*
WILLARD CLAY

tion — which plants are used for different-colored dyes; how a hogan is built, disassembled, and rebuilt many times using the same juniper logs; how Navajo dryland farmers trap water flowing down from the mesas to irrigate their watermelons, corn, and peach trees; how, if you stand close to a sandstone wall in a high wind, you can feel very fine sand particles pelting your face.

At noon we pull into a shady rock alcove at the head of a canyon where Kee sets up a cast-iron grate over a stick fire of piñon and juniper. Within a few minutes coffee is brewed, hamburgers sizzle on the grill, and a table is set with plates, cups, and condiments. Grilled-to-order burgers are consumed with gusto. Kee offers apples and cookies for dessert, and we're on our way again.

Although prolonged drought has driven many Navajo from the land, a few families still eke out an agricultural subsistence, hauling water for washing and drinking. We stop frequently to survey small Anasazi ruins in secluded places along the way. Often we find panels of rock art nearby.

Spring wildflowers bloom beside the single-track road. In places, shifting sands nearly bog us down, but the truck struggles through. Kee stops to point out something that has eluded everyone else's attention: "See the little hole at the bottom of the wall covered with sandstone bricks?" he asks. "That's where the old people stored some food."

In the late afternoon we drive toward the mouth of a small canyon. Tall cottonwood trees shade a compound consisting of a block house, corrals, a ramada, and a hogan made of juniper logs. A few horses wander about. There are lots of sheep.

The hogan, "home" in Navajo, has evolved over the years from a rounded, earth-covered, forked-stick dwelling to a six- or eight-sided structure made of cribbed logs or other materials. From primitive to modern, there are many variations in both style and construction materials. But whatever its construction, the hogan is more than a home or a place to work and socialize. Its shape, its orientation to the four cardinal directions, and even the conduct of life inside are reflections of Navajo philosophy.

The single door of the hogan always faces east, the most sacred point on the universal circle, which in Navajo mythology is the pattern of movement into and out of this world. The center of the interior, about 24 feet in diameter, is the cooking area with the smoke hole or chimney directly above it. Movement is clockwise around the center in keeping with the model of the universal circle. Traditionally, even the positioning of family members inside the dwelling is prescribed by Navajo concepts of universal patterns.

The hogan we stand before belongs to Kee's mother, a well-known Navajo weaver. We find her inside, sitting on a sheepskin laid over a dirt floor, working at her loom. To demonstrate the nature of her craft she cards some wool, spins it on a notched-stick spindle, then turns to her homemade upright loom to weave. Finished rugs of intricate design and color are displayed around the interior walls. Her work is exquisite.

While his mother works, Kee tells us that he grew up in a hogan very much like this one, in which a family of 12 lived quite comfortably. Water and firewood had to be collected. He knew nothing of electricity, indoor plumbing, or running water until he went away to Indian boarding school. "The Navajo people go to the higher mountains to get straight logs for hogans," he says. "The ones down here are too crooked." Another nugget for my notebook.

In the late afternoon we drive past Sun's Eye Arch where rock-art renderings show bighorn sheep leaping and frolicking on the walls, then past Ear of the Wind Arch, Big Hogan Arch, and Moccasin Arch. Rounding one end of Thunderbird Mesa, we find ourselves staring straight ahead at Totem Pole, a 400-foot sandstone minaret that in winter casts a shadow 8 miles long. We have come to a place that has become familiar to us through images flickering across movie and television screens. We have come to Monument Valley.

John Ford's *Stagecoach*, filmed in 1938, was the first movie shot on location in Monument Valley. Others include *My Darling Clementine* (1946); *The Searchers* (1956); *How the West Was Won* (1962); *The Trial of Billy Jack* (1973); *The Legend of the Lone Ranger* (1980), and of course countless television commercials. The Monument Valley Museum, housed in the original trading post adjacent to Goulding's Lodge, displays photographs and other motion-picture memorabilia, including a set from the John Wayne movie *She Wore a Yellow Ribbon*.

Ahead of us are Rain God Mesa, Camel Butte, East and West Mitten buttes, and all the other much-filmed sandstone formations of Monument Valley. Windswept and desolate, it's a harsh country, but transcendently beautiful too. Wind, rain, heat, cold, and shifting sand continue their work. The forces that sculpted these sandstone monoliths, "petrified sand dunes" of ancient seas, will in time wear them away to grains of sand.

(ABOVE) *The Three Sisters Buttes stand guard over a traditional earth-covered Navajo hogan.*
TOM TILL
(RIGHT) *The chill of winter adds an air of mystery to Monument Valley as an ethereal fog blankets the snow-covered basin.*
JACK DYKINGA

THE NAVAJO NATION

The precise date of Navajo settlement in Indian Country is unknown. The remains of a hogan found on Black Mesa date to around A.D. 1400, and some pottery remains that may or may not be Navajo date to an even earlier time. What we do know is that they were fairly well established by the time the Spaniards arrived in the middle of the 16th century. The first real proof of Navajo presence in the Four Corners region comes from the remains of a hut found in New Mexico, dating to about 1541. The Diné, as the Navajo people call themselves, settled among the already resident Pueblo Indians, intermingling with them and borrowing from Pueblo culture.

For the next several hundred years the Navajo fought for these lands. They fought against various Pueblo groups and against the Utes. They battled the Spaniards, then the Mexicans who gained independence from Spain in 1821, and finally the U.S. government, which took control of the Southwest in 1846.

In 1863, American soldiers led by Col. Kit Carson and Gen. James H. Carleton marched against the Navajo, killing livestock and burning fields and orchards. Many Navajo fled into remote canyons in isolated mountain ranges.

Those who did not, some 8,000 people, were marched 300 miles to Fort Sumner in New Mexico where they were held captive for five years.

In 1868 the U.S. Government signed a treaty with the Navajo and offered the tribe fertile lands, full of timber and game, in Oklahoma. They declined. Instead, the fewer than 6,000 survivors of the "Long Walk" elected to return to Dinétah, a 3.5-million acre reservation which was only a fraction of the land they had fought for in northeast Arizona.

Today, the Navajo Nation has grown to be the largest Indian tribe in the United States. Numbering more than 200,000, they occupy an area that Congress has expanded to a size larger than the state of West Virginia. While the 26,000-square-mile reservation lies mostly within

(ABOVE) *During World War II, Navajo Code Talkers, including Eugene Roanhorse Crawford (left) and Frank Thompson, confounded Japanese code breakers and contributed to the Allied victory.*
JERRY JACKA
(LEFT) *Rodeo action during the Navajo Fair at Chinle.*
MONTY ROESSEL

Arizona, it also spans parts of New Mexico and Utah. It is a nation of young people with more than 60 percent of the population under 24 years of age.

Tribal headquarters is in Window Rock, Arizona, beneath the red-stone arch for which the capitol is named. Historically significant in the Navajo Water Way Ceremony, the window is still important in Navajo religious observances.

Since 1938 the Navajo have elected a tribal council of 88 along with a tribal chairman and vice-chairman. Local government consists of 109 Chapter Houses throughout the reservation where "town meetings" are held to decide local issues and to approve recommendations to the tribal government itself.

The Navajo Nation Zoo and Botanical Park in Window Rock exhibits birds and animals native to the reservation. Also in Window Rock are the Navajo Arts and Crafts Enterprise and the Navajo Tribal Museum. The Navajo Nation Fair, the largest North American Indian fair, is held annually in September at the fairgrounds in Window Rock.

Navajo Community College, a two-year school in Tsaile, is the first community college in the United States owned and run by an Indian tribe. One of the main features of the college is the Ned Hatathli Cultural Center, a six-story building shaped like a hogan, that houses a museum and gallery showing Navajo arts and crafts.

Tribal revenues come principally from the sale of gas, oil, and coal, but Navajo reliance on extractive industries may be changing. Noting in a recent address that tourists come to Arizona for two reasons, "the Grand Canyon and the Indians," a tribal leader urged the tribe to become less dependent on non-renewable resources and to encourage tourism.

In addition to its natural wonders, the reservation features a busy calendar of events throughout the year. Rodeos and powwows, bike races, arts and crafts shows, song and dance festivals, and tribal-fairs are just some of the events that are open to the public.

(ABOVE) *His every step punctuated by bells, rattles, and drums, a young performer competes in the Navajo Nation Powwow.*
MONTY ROESSEL
(LEFT) *Shaped like a hogan, the ultra modern Hatathli Cultural Center of Navajo Community College reflects traditional values of the Navajo.*
GENE BALZER

◆ ◆ ◆ ◆ ◆

Canyon de Chelly

The wonders of this canyon cannot be fathomed in one visit, nor even two or three, but there are a couple of ways to get off to a promising start. One is to rent a ride in a big go-anywhere, Korean-War-vintage six-wheel-drive truck and explore the canyon bottomlands with a Navajo driver as guide. Another is to hire a guide to accompany you in your own four-wheel-drive vehicle. You can also go on foot, either by joining one of the daily hikes led by a Park Service ranger or by hiking into the canyon on your own along the White House Ruins Trail.

All-day truck tours and guided tours in your own four-wheel-drive vehicle travel both Canyon de Chelly and Canyon del Muerto extensively and take in White House, Sliding House, Antelope House, Mummy Cave, and other ruins and rock-art sites within the canyons. But for an intimate human-scale introduction to Canyon de Chelly's natural environment, hiking into the canyon from the White House Overlook is the way to go.

The trailhead for the 2.5-mile round-trip hike to the White House Ruins begins about 150 yards from White House Overlook parking lot on South Rim Drive 6.4 miles from the Visitors Center. Well-maintained, the trail is classified as moderately strenuous because it descends 600 feet to the canyon floor in slightly more than one mile. Hiking out can be exhausting.

◆ ◆ ◆ ◆ ◆

The weather is raw as I start to hike in solo from White House Overlook. A stiff breeze hurls occasional darts of icy rain against my face. Small wind-warped trees cling to the rim rock. The natural environment of the high-desert Colorado Plateau country is severe, and trees here are notably tough. In thin, shallow soils that hold little moisture, piñon, juniper, and scrub oak thrive in gale-force winds, winter temperatures well below freezing, and in summer heat and drought. With scaled, leathery leaves or short, stubby needles, these sturdy trees

(RIGHT) *From White House Overlook, Canyon de Chelly at first appears undisturbed. However, because the trail to White House is the only one that can be hiked without an official guide, this ruin is the most visited in the monument.*
DICK DIETRICH

are consummate water conservationists, and slow growth rates help them save energy.

As I drop below the rim I see cholla and prickly pear cacti, members of the family Opuntia, a class noted for its ability to withstand climatic extremes. Prickly pear, for example, covers a range that extends from Mexico north to southern British Columbia.

When land is overgrazed, alien plants quickly invade. Two such invaders, snakeweed and rabbit-brush, vivid green with yellow flowers, dot the landscape on the rim and beside the trail heading down. Pretty to look at, they taste terrible (snakeweed, tasting of turpentine, is poisonous to live-stock), so cows and other foragers usually leave them alone.

I keep my ears tuned. One of the pleasures of canyon hiking is the chorus of bird songs echoing down the walls. The descending trill of canyon wrens, the dolorous cooing of mourning doves, the rapid chatter of white-throated swifts, and the down-slurred scream of red-tailed hawks are familiar canyon sounds. Killdeers, ravens, golden eagles, nighthawks, turkey vultures, and great horned owls also live in canyon country.

Although daytime sightings are rare, mule deer, coyote, black bear, raccoon, mountain lion, bobcat, and badger are at home in Canyon de Chelly. On this chilly day the only mammal showing its face is a rock squirrel, the biggest of Arizona's ground squirrels, whose bell-like alarm call had me search-ing my field guides in vain for a bird call to match before I discov-ered the source of that incessant pinging.

The gray wolf, grizzly bear, Merriam's elk, bighorn sheep, and pronghorn — all now extirpated from the canyon — once roamed here. Two that were wiped out, the wild turkey and the beaver, have been reintroduced in out-of-the-way canyon locations. The many rock-art drawings of turkeys suggest they were once an important part of the Anasazi culture.

Descending, I can clearly see in the canyon walls what I have previously learned about Canyon de Chelly's geology. Two hundred million years ago a great desert blanketed this region and the outlines of its sand dunes are still visible. The dunes accu-mulated to many hundreds of feet. Other materials laid down over them through geologic ages com-pressed them to rock. In time, uplifting forces frac-tured the Earth's crust into cracks and faults. Erosion finished the job, deepening and widening these fissures to create the canyonlands of Canyon de Chelly.

Unlike the drought-adapted oak, juniper, and piñon pine on the rim, the trees and shrubs of Canyon de Chelly's bottomlands are typical of desert riparian flora. The dominant native trees are water-loving cottonwood and willow, with netleaf hackberry, chokecherry, and box elder growing in the side canyons.

Russian olive, peach-leaf willow, salt cedar, and tamarisk — exotics introduced for erosion control — flourish throughout the canyons. Carrizo, a native grass resembling cane and much prized as a

(ABOVE) *Appearing like a sundial for the gods, Spider Rock rises more than 830 feet from the floor of Canyon de Chelly.*
PETER KRESAN
(LEFT) *Antelope House, at the base of a 630-foot wall, is named for Indian pictographs of the animals that once roamed here in numbers.*
WILLARD CLAY

material for thatching, arrow shafts, twine, and matting, grows in dense thickets in some canyon locations.

Near the foot of the trail I come upon a hogan and a small Navajo farm. In canyon-bottom orchards attended by Navajo farmers I'm surprised to find peach, apricot, and plum trees, which were brought into the region by the Spanish and introduced into the canyon by Hopi gardeners in the seventeenth century. Starting with the Anasazi nearly 2,000 years ago, Native Americans have

always farmed the canyon bottomlands in summer, growing melons, squash, corn, and beans. Today, Navajo drive flocks of sheep from winter pasture on the rim to summer pasture in the canyon bottom where forage and water are more dependable.

Wading the wash, I come to Kini-na-a-kai, White House, a name derived from the white plastered walls at the top of the ruin. Along with Mummy Cave Ruin in Canyon del Muerto, White House Ruin is the best-known of the many pueblos in the Canyon de Chelly region.

An impressive ruin that once contained up to 80 rooms and four kivas and housed as many as 40 people, White House is curiously lacking in rock art. On the cliff face behind the lower ruin there is a man with raised arms, a star shape, a few concentric circles and other abstract designs — that's all.

Looking up at White House, I lean against the trunk of a cottonwood. A chill wind rattles its branches. I imagine ancient sounds — the sounds of children playing, of women chatting around cooking fires, of beating drums and deep voices rising from kivas, and of the village crier announcing the news of the day from the highest roof. "All is well," I hear him call. "All is well."

(TOP, LEFT) *Mummy Cave Ruin.* JOHN DREW
(TOP, RIGHT) *The arrangement of "stars" found on the ceiling of this small cave are a unique example of ancient rock art.*
JERRY JACKA
(ABOVE) *These Navajo charcoal drawings, dated to the early 1800s, record the arrival of Lt. Antonio Narbona and his Spanish troops.*
JERRY JACKA

Canyon de Chelly, pronounced "d'Shay," is probably a Spanish corruption of the Navajo word *tségi,* meaning "rock canyon," or "in a canyon." The first Anglo-American description, written by Lt. James H. Simpson in 1849, refers to it as "Cañon of Chelly" or "Cañon de Chai." The natural beauty of Canyon de Chelly and its hundreds of cliff dwellings and rock-art sites repeatedly struck Lieutenant Simpson as "stupendous."

Throughout the canyons the array of pictographs and petroglyphs overwhelms the senses. Most of the rock art is Anasazi in origin, but the Navajo have added to these displays with their own original style. A few of the paintings and etchings may be Hopi (descendants of the Anasazi), who were sporadic canyon dwellers until the Navajo took over for good in the mid-1700s.

By far the largest rock-art display is the 75-foot horizontal panel called The Wall or Newspaper Rock. Turkeys, deer, ducks, bird-headed men, legless humans with triangular bodies, flute players, and an assortment of spirals and other abstractions cover the wall. Most of these figures, scratched or pecked onto the dark patina of desert varnish, are Anasazi. The horse and rider petroglyphs and those of men with shields are Navajo.

Navajo rock-art style consists of lifelike, energetic drawings of objects from daily life — cows, deer, pronghorns, birds. On the ceilings of some caves, often more than ten feet from the floor, are very carefully painted stars. At least 32 of these "planetaria" have been counted.

Navajo paintings frequently represent historical events. At Standing Cow Ruin in Canyon del Muerto a mural shows a line of Spanish horsemen. The central figure, wearing a black cape and carrying a cross, may be Lt. Antonio Narbona, who led a Spanish expedition against the Navajo in 1804-05, killing many Navajo men, women, and children at a site called Massacre Cave. The Ute Raid Panel in Canyon del Muerto depicts a fight in 1858 between the Navajo and invading Utes.

Whether you walk into Canyon de Chelly with a park ranger, hike on your own into White House Ruin, take a guided tour in a four-wheel-drive vehicle, ride horseback with an authorized Navajo guide, or drive the rim of Canyon de Chelly and Canyon del Muerto in your automobile — do it once and you'll want to return again and again.

◆ **Canyon de Chelly National Monument**
   P.O. Box 588
   Chinle, AZ 86503
   602-674-5500

◆ **Canyon de Chelly Thunderbird Tours**
   P.O. Box 2217
   Chinle, AZ 86503
   602-674-5841 or 674-5842

JERRY SIEVE

FOUR CORNERS

It's the only place in the United States where the borders of four separate states — Arizona, Utah, Colorado, and New Mexico — actually touch. There's a precise spot, marked by the Four Corners Monument, where you can lean down and put one limb in the corner of each state. It's a little awkward, but you're straddling all four states at the same time.

I felt sheepish, but I did it. Everybody does. While I was there a tour leader lined up a group of well-dressed Japanese tourists and had them take turns standing on the marker and photographing each other. While watching them, I heard a loud roar and turned to see 12 road-hardened members of a Chicago motorcycle club — all chains and leather and bulging biceps — rumbling up the road on big Harley-Davidson "hogs." A few minutes later they too were standing on the monument, grinning like chimps and saying "cheese" for the camera.

But Four Corners is more than a cartographic oddity. Historically, culturally, and geographically it is unique. The Spanish Conquistadors considered the entire region an extension of their New Mexico empire. The great Pueblo Indian cultures, still intact on the Hopi Mesas and along the Rio Grande, consider this region sacred. And the landforms hereabout — high plateaus, canyons, buttes, and mesas — are like no others. It's easy to understand why five national parks and 18 national monuments lie within a 150-mile radius of the Four Corners Monument.

Chapter 4 ◆ Indian Country

HOPILAND

This is the lay of the land. Rising to more than 7,600 feet on the Colorado Plateau south of U.S. Route 160 near the small Navajo community of Tsegi, Black Mesa sprawls south and east across Indian Country for more than 60 miles.

Picture Black Mesa as the heel of a giant hand with several finger-like projections branching toward the southwest. Close to Black Mesa's southern terminus at Black Mountain, three of these fingers probe for many miles into the desert before ending abruptly where State Route 264 snakes around, over, and through the buttes, mesas, and pinnacles of this bleak, arid landscape. At the very tips of these three jagged fingers, settled lightly atop sheer cliffs rising more than 600 feet above the desert floor, are the weathered hand-hewn stone and mud-plaster dwellings of the Hopi villages. One of these villages, Old Oraibi on Third Mesa, may be the oldest continuously inhabited village in the United States. It is thought to have been settled about A.D. 1150.

Strung out along State Route 264 from Moenkopi in the west (next to Tuba City) to Keams Canyon 80 miles east, are several Hopi villages. Hotevilla, Old Oraibi, Kykotsmovi (also known as "New Oraibi"), and Bacabi are anchored to Third Mesa 45 miles east of Moenkopi. Shungopavi, Shipaulovi, and Mishongnovi are located on Second Mesa. And Hano, Sichomovi, Polacca, and Walpi are on First Mesa. The mesas themselves are tightly clustered, with the road distance between First and Third mesas being only about 12 miles.

In Hopi mythology these landforms, which encompass only a few hundred square miles and are virtually engulfed by the much larger Navajo reservation, are Tuwanasavi, the Center of the Earth, the Sacred Circle, the holiest of places. Many of the important symbols and icons of Hopi religious belief are visible from the mesas. Corn Rock, with its twin spires jutting into the air near a small graveyard below the Second Mesa village of Mishongnovi, is in full view from many places as you travel around Hopiland.

The sacred peaks of the San Francisco mountains, more than 80 miles away, loom large on the southwest horizon. Kachina deities are believed to live high among these peaks. They visit the Hopi villages each year, starting at the time of the winter solstice. In the months that follow they bring rain to the fields and orchards below the mesas and preside over the production and distribution of the harvest. At summer solstice, when the sun again turns south, the kachinas return to the peaks.

◆ ◆ ◆ ◆ ◆

Rising early, we breakfast on blue-cornmeal pancakes in the restaurant at the Hopi Cultural Center and Motel on Second Mesa. It's Monday morning, springtime, and in the sun-bright air the fields below the mesas lie ready for planting. Small orchards of apple, pear, apricot, and peach are radiant with pink and white blossoms.

Around 9 A.M. we come to the villages of First

(LEFT) *Pickup trucks are one of the few modern conveniences found at the Hopi village of Walpi.*
JERRY JACKA

Mesa, driving the winding road that skirts the mesa's steep escarpment to within a quarter-mile of the summit and hiking the rest of the way up. As we enter the village of Hano, a young man calls from his doorway to ask if we want to see some kachina carvings or pottery. Our goal is Walpi, the village perched out on the edge of the mesa, so we decline his invitation and promise to stop on the way back.

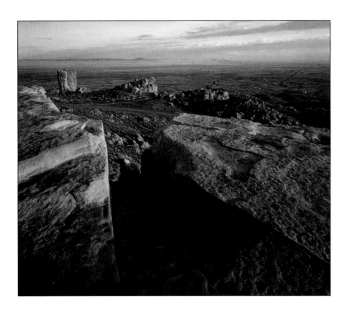

(TOP) *This ancient stairway was once the main access route to the Second Mesa villages. Corn Rock can be seen just beyond the road. On the plain below are modern dwellings funded by the U.S. Department of Housing and Urban Development.*
JERRY JACKA
(RIGHT) *In Hopi belief, ceremonies are vital to ensure the harmony of man and Nature. Here, Butterfly Dancers perform at Second Mesa.*
JERRY JACKA
(ABOVE) *Houses in the Hopi village of Moenkopi are as angular and low slung as the mesas that surround them.*
JAMES TALLON

At the middle village, Sichomovi, Hopi for "flower-hill place," we come to an open square anchored by a community building, Punsi Hall. A sign above the entrance directs all tourists to stop and register. Inside, we are greeted by a young woman who tells us that in a few minutes she'll be leading a tour through Sichomovi and into Walpi.

A placard on the wall above her desk lists rules for guests: no picture-taking, no audio-visual recording, no disturbing or removing of objects from the villages. Centuries of contact have taught the Hopi that outsiders break the rules repeatedly, so before starting the tour, our guide asks visitors carrying cameras to leave them in a locked cabinet.

Bundles of prayer feathers sprout like bouquets beside the road, evidence of an important ceremonial dance at Walpi on Sunday, the day before. We had planned to enter Walpi on that Sunday, but were stopped by a sign at the base of the mesa: "Non-Indians not allowed during ceremonials."

"But we're the good guys," I wanted to say, "well-behaved, polite, we'll stay in the background, keep quiet, mind our manners." But such signs are posted for good reason. Many non-Indian spectators violate sacred Hopi ceremonial dances by sneaking in cameras and tape recorders, talking loudly, or dressing in a manner the Hopi consider inappropriate for holy occasions. Moreover, the villages are small, there are no public facilities, and sometimes there isn't even room for all the Hopi who want to attend. Disappointed, we turned back.

Today, as we walk through Sichomovi, an acrid odor floats on the light morning breeze. Someone is firing pottery in an open kiln fueled by sheep dung. Hand-lettered signs tacked above the thresholds of some houses offer kachina carvings or pottery for sale. As we pass, some residents hurry out to post "open" signs. Traditionally, some of the best Hopi pottery is crafted on First Mesa. Tewa-speaking Rio Grande Pueblo Indians, highly skilled pot makers, settled here after the Pueblo Revolt against the Spaniards in 1680. Over time they learned the Hopi language and adopted Hopi ways and are now thoroughly assimilated into Hopi culture.

To walk across the narrow rock isthmus that separates Sichomovi from Walpi ("place of the gap") is to step back in time. Our guide tells us that Walpi lacks running water and electricity and is inhabited by only a few "old ones." Although they now get their water from a faucet located just the other side of the gap instead of having to haul it up hundreds of steep, stone-carved steps from springs at the base of the mesa, Walpi's residents still live the old way, cooking and heating on wood fires and baking in beehive ovens in their yards.

Many of Walpi's dwellings were saved from ruin by a federally funded restoration project. With its empty lanes and overall appearance of vacancy, the village has a picturesque, movie-set aura. But Walpi comes alive during important ritual performances. At those times its plaza is thronged with visitors from other villages who come to watch the day-long ceremonial dances.

◆　◆　◆　◆　◆

Maj. John Wesley Powell, the man who led the first expedition by boat through the Grand Canyon, visited the Hopi mesas in 1870. Five years later, writing carefully detailed observations about his experiences for *Scribner's Monthly*, Powell notes, "The people are very hospitable and quite ceremonious." Elsewhere he says, "They are also very polite. If you meet them out in their fields, they salute you with a greeting which seems to mean, 'May the birds sing happy songs in your fields.'"

The word Hopi means "well-behaved, well-mannered," and anyone who has spent time in the villages can attest to these traits. But in describing the Hopi as "ceremonious," Major Powell, I assume, meant "formal and dignified," which also explains the Hopi attitude toward outsiders.

Too often visitors respond to Hopi hospitality in ways that are "unceremonious" — rude or undigni-

fied — and hospitality is withdrawn. At the entrance of Old Oraibi on Third Mesa a sign long stood that read, "Warning, Warning. No outside white visitors allowed because of your failure to obey the laws of our tribe as well as the laws of your own. This village is hereby closed." The last time I visited Old Oraibi, the sign had been removed and I was permitted to walk freely about the village. But I won't be surprised if it is put back.

In many respects Hopi communities are autonomous village-states, so the question of whether or not to admit tourists is a local issue. While most ceremonial dances are off-limits to non-Indians, tourists are sometimes allowed to witness social dances.

So perhaps it is best to go to the Hopi mesas with an open heart and an open mind. Don't expect anything. Visit the Cultural Center, browse the arts and crafts shops, stroll through Walpi or some other villages, and enjoy the stupendous scenery. If you are invited to observe a dance, or asked into a Hopi home and catch a glimmer of insight into Hopi life, consider it the privilege that it is.

(ABOVE) *In addition to its food value, corn is used extensively in religious ceremonies. The Hopi are noted for their "dryland farming" techniques, raising good crops in a desert environment.* CHRISTINE KEITH

◆ **Hopi Cultural Center**
P.O. Box 67
Second Mesa, AZ 86043
602-734-2401

TRADING POSTS

In most of Indian Country's bigger towns, with their supermarkets, department store catalog outlets, auto-parts stores, and fast-food palaces, trading posts are already gone. Garcia's Trading Post in Chinle is now a shell of a building, its walls scrawled with graffiti. The original trading post at the mouth of Canyon de Chelly is now the dining room at the Thunderbird Lodge; Goulding's at Monument Valley has become a museum. The Wide Ruins and Black Mountain trading posts are no more — burned to the ground — and the demise of the trading post at Tolchacho was sealed when a new bridge built across the Little Colorado River in 1934 bypassed its location at Old Leupp.

The posts that survived the greater mobility of reservation Indians, made possible by improved roads and pickup trucks and the ensuing transition from bartering and pawn to a cash economy, are either located on well-travelled roads sustained by a lively tourist trade or are far enough off the beaten path to still function as real trading posts. Falling into the first category are Cameron, Tuba, Keams Canyon, the new McGee's Beyond Native Tradition Gallery in Holbrook, and the famous Hubbell Trading Post in Ganado, now a National Historic Site. The posts at Shonto, Salinas Springs, Rock Point, Woodsprings, Burntwater, and Many Farms fall into the latter category.

Early trading posts were often no more than flat-roofed sheds slapped together with native materials. Some traders even operated for a time out of tents. The trader usually worked behind a counter to one side of the room while his customers gathered in the "bull pen" in the center to smoke free tobacco, play cards, exchange news, or haggle with the trader.

Indians traded wool, baskets, blankets, rugs, jewelry, and even livestock for coffee, salt, flour, bacon, potatoes, oats, peanuts, saddles, rifles, canned foods, dry goods, calico, shoes, hats, velveteen, cookware, knives, needles and thread, and sometimes even instruction by the trader's wife in such skills as how to run a sewing machine.

Often a man of many parts, the trader served as doctor, arbiter of disputes, and undertaker. And he was also quite likely an agent for Indian artisans, helping to peddle their wares to markets far from the reservation.

John Lorenzo Hubble was the embodiment of the successful trader who began trading in Ganado in 1876 and two years later bought the post that still bears his name. Hubbell was much more than a trader to the Navajo, whose language and

customs he took great care to learn. Known as "Double Glasses" for his thick round eyeglasses, he became a trusted friend.

By all accounts he was a square dealer who treated Indians with respect and dignity. He wrote letters for them, explained government policy, and helped settle conflicts. When a smallpox epidemic hit the reservation, Hubbell converted his home to a hospital and worked night and day administering to the sick.

Hubbell once said, "The first duty of an Indian trader . . . is to look after the material welfare of his neighbors; to advise them to produce that which their natural inclinations and talent best adapts them; to treat them honestly and insist upon getting the same treatment from them...to find a market for their products and vigilantly watch that they keep improving in the production of same . . . ." By insisting that they "keep improving," Hubbell helped to refine Navajo silversmithing and rug weaving into highly accomplished art forms.

But J. L. Hubbell was neither missionary nor altruist. "The trader," he said, "should [not] forget that he is here to see that he makes a fair profit for himself." But he added a qualification that reveals something of the character of the man: "for whatever would injure him would naturally injure those with whom he comes in contact."

Hubbell ran the post at Ganado for 50 years and, along with his sons, at one time owned and operated 24 trading posts and other businesses in Indian Country. When he died in 1930 he was buried on nearby Hubbell Hill in a grave next to his wife, Lina Rubi, and his best friend among the Navajo, Many Horses. Mourning his loss, one Navajo man said:

You wear out your shoes, you buy another pair;
You gather melons, and more will grow on the vine;
You grind corn to make bread,
*   and next year you have plenty more corn;*
But my friend Don Lorenzo is gone,
*   and none to take his place.*

(**ABOVE, LEFT**) *The entrance to the Hubbell Trading Post is marked by this sun-bleached cow skull and carved Indian image.*
JERRY JACKA
(**ABOVE**) *Pioneer trader John Lorenzo Hubbell's home is now a National Historic Site.*
JERRY JACKA
(**LEFT**) *The old Hubbell Trading Post is still open for business.*
GEORGE H.H. HUEY
(**RIGHT**) *Old trade tokens bear the names of the establishments where they were legal tender.*
GENE BALZER

◆ **Hubbell Trading Post Historic Site**
P.O. Box 150
Ganado, AZ 86505
602-755-3475

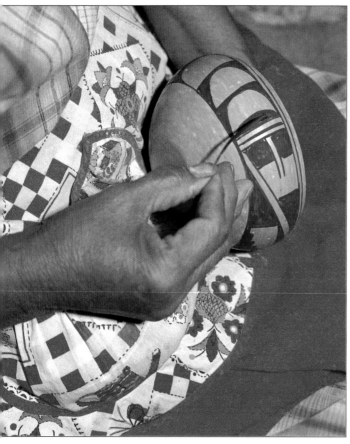

INDIAN ARTS & CRAFTS

Basket weaving and pottery are two Native American art forms that extend far back in time. More recently, the creativity and adaptability of Hopi and Navajo artists are best illustrated by the story of how silversmithing took root and flourished among them.

It begins with the Navajo who, at first, were not interested in working silver because it was easier to trade a horse or sheep for a few coveted trinkets offered by itinerant Mexican *plateros*, travelling silversmiths.

In the early 1850s a Navajo named Atsidi Sani (Old Smith) learned the basics of silver working from one of these men. Its popularity as a craft, however, did not immediately become widespread. During the Navajo's captivity in New Mexico, some learned blacksmithing. This may explain why more of them took up silversmithing when they returned to the Four Corners area in 1868.

(CLOCKWISE FROM TOP LEFT)
"Old pawn" silver concha belts can carry price tags of $1,500.
TOM TILL
Navajo weaver Ruth Ann Tracey creates an intricate pattern using muted desert colors.
JERRY JACKA
These necklaces of turquoise, coral, and hundreds of "hishi" beads are dated to the late 1800s.
JERRY JACKA
Using a yucca fiber brush, Vivian Mumzewa decorates pottery the way her Hopi ancestors did.
JERRY JACKA

About 1872 one of these silver workers, Atsidi Chon (Ugly Smith), a son of Old Smith, taught his craft to members of the Zuñi tribe in exchange for livestock. The Zuñi, in turn, taught the Hopi. Thus, by the end of the 19th century, silversmithing was well established among both the Navajo and Hopi.

In the beginning, the raw material was silver coins, which the Indians hammered flat, then cut, shaped, and finished or sometimes melted and poured into molds. Concha belts and belt buckles were produced in this manner. American coins were used until 1890 when it became illegal to melt them down. This bothered few craftsmen because the Mexican peso was preferred for its higher silver content and greater malleability.

When Mexico banned the export of its coins in 1930, Indian silver workers used silver ingots, melting them down to turn out buttons, beads, bracelets, rings, buckles, and other items. In addition to silver, craftsmen also fashioned items from brass and copper salvaged from discarded pots and pans.

Traders helped shape the art form of silversmithing by hiring Mexican silversmiths to instruct Indian jewelers, and by purchasing silver in ready-to-work sheets and wire coils.

In addition to the turquoise beads and nuggets that had been used for hundreds of years in jewelery and other body adornment, Indian craftsmen were encouraged by traders to use cut stone imported from Persia. The traders also furnished trade beads, garnets, and bits of colored glass obtained from broken earrings and pieces of jewelry. In time, as more mines opened in the Southwest, and with them more lapidary shops, Native American artists found local sources for cut and polished stone.

Early Indian silver work was traded solely among Native Americans. But by the late 1890s, the development of the railroad brought tourists to Indian country and new markets burgeoned for arts and handicrafts. Soon Navajo and Hopi artisans were filling orders for cuff links, tie bars, and pendants. Some of these items were stamped with thunderbirds and swastikas to cater to Easterner notions of "authenticity." When tourists asked to know the "symbolism" of a running horse or a cloud pattern, enterprising merchants satisfied the demand with a list of meanings.

Along the way, Navajo artists, great learners and adapters, made other changes. Sandcasting, an Indian application of local materials to an old technology, is a good example. Volcanic tuff, a porous stone that is heat-resistant but soft enough to work

surface brushed with fine steel wool for contrast.

Once Hopi jewelers learned to produce overlay, they made it distinctively Hopi, applying petroglyph motifs and stylized animal figures and other designs borrowed from Hopi textiles, pottery, and basketry. Some artists even stamped intricate designs into the recessed areas of the jewelry. Today, Hopi and many other Indian jewelers are adept at silver overlay work.

The same kinds of innovation are evident in Indian weaving, basketry, pottery, painting, sculpting, and carving. In producing their arts and crafts, creative Navajo and Hopi, like artists everywhere, respond to influences within and outside their cultures. But perhaps more important to growth and change as artists, they respond to their own creative urges — their unique visions and inspirations.

with a knife, was used to make matching halves of a design mold. The halves were then clamped tightly together and molten silver poured into a funnel shape at one end. When the silver cooled and hardened, the finished piece was removed and polished.

The development of overlay silver work among the Hopi illustrates how a learned technique can evolve into a distinctive style. For a long time Hopi and Navajo jewelry-making developed side by side, one style indistinguishable from the other. Then in the late 1930s the Museum of Northern Arizona began to offer "silver overlay" instruction to Hopi jewelers. This technique required a design be cut into one silver sheet and then overlaid onto a second undecorated surface and soldered into place. The recessed area is then oxidized and the outer

(LEFT) *Hopi overlay silver work, some with a touch of gold, incorporates traditional symbols into modern designs.*
(ABOVE) *Navajo artisan Perry Shorty surrounds bold splashes of turquoise with intricate silver work.*
(RIGHT, ABOVE) *Vibrant-hued symbols of nature often adorn Hopi basketry, which is widely noted for its quality workmanship.*
(RIGHT) *Hopi pottery is prized for its depiction of life forms and detailed geometric patterns.*
ALL BY JERRY JACKA

Early kachina carvings, for example, concentrated on the mask and headpiece, paying little attention to body detail. Eventually, carvers put more care into the arms and legs and began to convey action in their figures, much like the motions of dancers who represent the kachina deities in ceremonies. In time, realistic proportions were imparted to the carvings with the painstaking detail paid to costumes and painting.

Today, kachina carvers create amazingly bold figures, vividly painted, full of action and display. Fashioned from cottonwood roots, kachina carvings are representational, but can be impressionistic, bordering on the abstract. Now it is possible to look at a kachina and identify its carver by the distinctiveness of its conception and execution.

The influence of Indian traders on the development of Indian arts and crafts, particularly Navajo rug weaving, was powerful. It was once possible, for instance, to identify a Navajo rug-weaving style by its place of origin, often owing to the influence of a trading post in that place. Thus, buyers could say with certainty that a particular rug came from Ganado, Wide Ruins, or Two Grey Hills. But just as the globe has been shrunk by telecommunications, reservations have been shrunk by paved roads and pickups. Nowadays, a rug in the Teec Nos Pos style might be woven in Ganado.

Increasingly, young people leave reservations to study art formally at such places as the Institute of American Indian Art, started with a Rockefeller grant at the University of Arizona and continued in Santa Fe, New Mexico. The result is that much Navajo and Hopi art goes beyond traditional forms and material. Now, it may be more accurate to describe many carvers, sculptors, jewelers, potters, silversmiths, painters, and weavers as artists who happen to be Indian rather than as Indian artists.

Surely none of them would balk at being identified as Indian artists, for it is their culture that nurtures and inspires their work and stamps it with the singular qualities that distinguish it from the arts and crafts of other cultures.

(BELOW) *Hopi kachina carvings are one of the most recognized forms of Native American art. They range from the rough cut and sparsely adorned, to elaborate figures with intricate detail.*
JERRY JACKA

BUYING INDIAN ARTS AND CRAFTS

Buying Indian art can be a daunting experience. On the reservations, it seems to be everywhere, with prices ranging from a few dollars for a pair of earrings to several thousand dollars for a tapestry-quality Navajo weaving. So the inexperienced consumer is left to wonder: Where do I look? How can I tell if it's really Indian? What questions do I ask? How much should I pay?

While not a comprehensive guide, these suggestions may help you feel more comfortable while selecting and purchasing Indian arts and crafts.

◆In Chapter 1 I recommended a visit to the Museum of Northern Arizona for background on Indian arts and crafts. The same may be said for the Heard Museum in Phoenix; Arizona State Museum at the University of Arizona, Tucson; and the Amerind Foundation and Museum near Dragoon, Arizona. Staff members are knowledgeable about arts and crafts and can answer your questions. In addition, the gift shops of these museums offer a selection of books on the subject.

◆Even with little experience, you can tell a lot by closely examining the work. When selecting a piece of jewelry, for example, examine it for cracks or careless soldering. If stones are inlaid, check to see if they have been carefully cut and polished. If the piece is stamped, examine it for evenness of impression. In looking at a rug, note the intricacy of the design and check the tightness of the weave. A rug with a tighter weave (the number of warp and weft threads per inch) will cost more because it took longer to weave. Check to see if the rug is handspun or commer-cially spun. If you can't tell, ask. The harder you look and the more questions you ask, the more informed your decisions will be.

◆Don't swallow misleading claims. While they may add to the cost because it takes more time to procure and prepare them, plant dyes in rugs, for example, are no more authentic than aniline dyes. Both methods of dyeing have been used by Navajo weavers for a long time. More important than the type of dye used is the uniformity of color.

◆Unless you are secure in your own judgments, shop only at reputable trading posts and galleries. Ask traders and gallery owners for advice, especially when it involves making a decision about a specialty item, such as a Hopi kachina carving or something costly. As experience refines your judgment you may want to venture from the beaten path and deal directly with Indian artists and craftsmen.

(ABOVE) *Opportunities to buy arts and crafts spring up along reservation roadsides. Learning what to look for when buying a particular craft lays the groundwork for a wise investment.* P.K. WEIS

Chapter 6 ◆ *Indian Country*

PETRIFIED FOREST NATIONAL PARK

They were the Warrior Twins of the Sun and Changing Woman (sometimes called White Shell Woman), and their heroic quest was to seek out and slay Yé'iitsoh, Big Giant. Yé'iitsoh was the largest and fiercest of the monsters that preyed upon the Navajo people. With help from Spider Woman, who gave them a magic song to protect them and guide their footsteps, the Twins overcame dangerous obstacles to seek counsel from their father, Jóhonaa'éí, the Sun, at his home in the east.

After testing the Twins in a grueling series of physical trials to satisfy himself that they were indeed his sons, Jóhonaa'éí armed them with chain- and sheet-lightning arrows, sunbeam and rainbow arrows, and to each he gave a stone knife with a hard blade and a stone knife with a broad blade. With their weapons and suits of flint armor reflecting streaks of fire and lightning, the fearsome twin warriors went forth to fight Yé'iitsoh, Big Giant.

The Twins first caught sight of Yé'iitsoh as he was down on all fours drinking from a lake. When the young warriors saw that Big Giant had almost drained the lake in four gulps, they were afraid. But when the monster threatened to eat them, they recovered their courage and mocked him. Dodging lightning bolts hurled at them by Big Giant, the brothers unleashed their own arsenal of weapons.

Sparks and shards of flint armor flew as the Twins' lightning arrows struck and killed Yé'iitsoh. The Twins lopped off Big Giant's head and blood flowed everywhere, staining the ground in patterns of light and dark.

Thereafter, the older of the Twins was called Naayéé'neizghání, Monster Slayer. In time, Monster Slayer tracked down and killed all the monsters, while his younger brother (Tó Bájísh Chini, Child Born For Water) stayed home to protect the lodge. When Naayéé'neizghání, Monster Slayer, brought hair, feathers, eyes and other battle trophies to the Sun, his father, Jóhonaa'éí, commanded that the bodies of all the monsters be brought to one place and buried properly beneath ground stained by the blood of Yé'iitsoh.

The bones of these monsters now lie everywhere on the ground. And it is other body parts hacked off in battle — toes, scales, bits of feather, claws — that we sometimes find sticking from mud and rocks, not fossils, as some think.

— Navajo Creation Myth
on the Painted Desert

While not precisely the monsters of Navajo legends, monsters did indeed once roam what is now Petrified Forest National Park. The park is located in the southernmost reach of the Painted Desert which extends along the valley of the Little Colorado River between Holbrook and the Grand Canyon.

Picture, if you can, this desert as swamp. It is the Triassic period, 200 million years ago, a time of gargantuan reptiles, some with armor-plated bodies

(LEFT) *Logs of petrified wood collect in the crevices of Blue Mesa while other sections of these stone giants remain perched on precarious pedestals.*
RANDY PRENTICE

measuring up to 30 feet long, rows of large flesh-rending teeth, and the ability to rear up on their hind legs and run down prey in short, powerful sprints.

It is a time, too, of giant fern-like trees towering to 250 feet in a tropical climate. Wet and warm, its rivers, streams, marshes, and ponds teem with clams, mollusks, fishes, and gigantic amphibians. But it is an eerie world, a world without flowers, grasses, or birds. These will not evolve for more than 100 million years.

Felled by violent tropical storms that sometimes destroy vast tracts of forest, or done in by disease or old age, many giant trees topple into slow-moving rivers, then float into swamps or backwaters and are buried beneath layers of mud. Cut off from oxygen by tons of silt, the trees stop decomposing.

Meanwhile, above the graveyard of giant trees, powerful volcanic eruptions spew plumes of ash into the atmosphere. Gradually, the ash settles to the surface and sinks through the mud sediments where, over eons, minerals infiltrate the buried logs, replacing wood cells with crystals of many colors — red and rust from iron, blue and blue-green from copper, black from carbon and manganese, white and gray from quartz. The wood turns to stone.

Time passes. Crushed by the weight of rock strata, the buried logs crack into pieces. Upthrusting, tilting, and fracturing of the Earth's crust splinter still more of the entombed behemoths. Gradually over millennia the colossal Colorado Plateau rises, and the Painted Desert as we know it emerges.

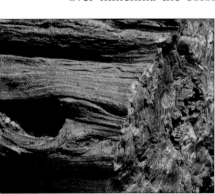

Cycles of sun, wind, and rain wear away black lava to uncover softer rock. These mudstones, claystones, siltstones, and sandstones erode more easily. As they wear away, fragments of petrified wood, plant, and animal fossils are

(ABOVE) *The gem-like quality of petrified wood is illuminated in the afternoon light.*
JACK DYKINGA
(RIGHT) *Erosion has exposed the clearly defined strata at the Little Painted Desert County Park north of Winslow.*
TOM BEAN

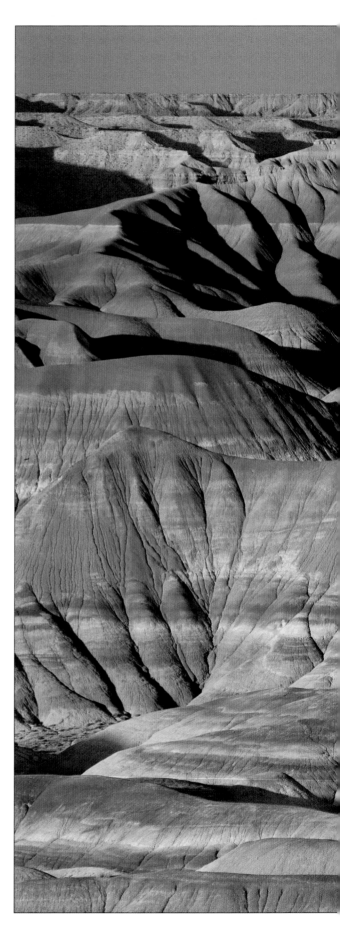

exposed to the light of day again. Still, today, the process continues as wind and rain erode fine-grained rock to reveal more of the past.

◆　◆　◆　◆　◆

But the Painted Desert and Petrified Forest are more than colored earth and giant trees turned to stone during grand-scale climatological and geological changes. They are about human history too. Although only a nanosecond in the long, slow pulse of geologic time, human history goes back at least 10,000 years when big-game hunters roamed the region. More advanced cultures followed, leaving behind potsherds, spear points, and tools as evidence of their existence.

More than 200 sites for human habitation, ranging from pithouses to small pueblos and kivas, have been found in the Petrified Forest. During the peak of human activity, around A.D. 1075 to 1125, groups of people lived in fairly large pueblos near washes and rivers. Eventually, however, the prolonged drought which began about A.D. 1150 forced them to move on.

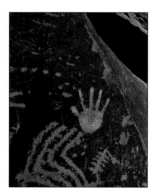

Puerco Ruin, a 76-room Anasazi pueblo in the Petrified Forest, was one of the last to be abandoned. On tumbled boulders nearby, petroglyphs — drawings of spirals, circles, stick figures and abstract designs — are pecked into dark stains on the rocks.

One of the most interesting of these petroglyphs is a solstice marker created by the villagers of the Puerco River Pueblo — a solar calendar which to this day silently signals the beginning of summer.

As people left the region, perhaps bound for the Hopi Mesas 60 miles north, one of their last stops may have been Homolovi, "Place of the Mounds," the state park near Winslow that once consisted of six pueblos housing hundreds of people. Hopi clan members still visit Homolovi to pray for the spirits of the *hisatsinom*, the "old people long ago."

◆　◆　◆　◆　◆

The only way to truly feel the Petrified Forest is to hike into it. And yet walking through this bizarre polychrome geometry of multilayered cones, slumped cliffs, and rain-slashed gullies of constantly shifting terrain can befuddle the senses and have you half-believing (or wanting to believe) that the bones of monsters are indeed scattered here.

Petrified wood, from thumbnail-size chips to logs several feet long — the largest concentration to be

(**ABOVE, LEFT**) *One of the petroglyphs on Newspaper Rock is the imprint of the artist.*
GILL C. KENNY
(**ABOVE**) *Generally shy, pronghorn antelope can often be seen grazing on distant ridges.*
CHUCK PLACE
(**LEFT**) *Called Puerco Ruins for the nearby river of the same name, these slab and mud dwellings were abandoned some time before A.D. 1400.*
GARY LADD

found anywhere in the world — is strewn every-where, and recently exposed nuggets, blocks, and slabs of the stuff quite literally fall out of eroding cliffs almost every day.

Petrified wood is one of the densest materials you will ever heft in the palm of your hand. A chunk the size of a good-sized navel orange feels like a 16-pound cannon shot, and it will not surprise you to learn that a cubic foot weighs 175 pounds. When seen from the proper angle the facets of its jeweled surface flare to kaleidoscopic brilliance.

Follow a stream bed up one of the dry washes of the region's watershed. Examine the filigree of ani-mal and bird tracks in the sticky clay and soft sands; note the trees, shrubs, and grasses growing in the riparian channel itself. You will begin to understand that, badland though it may be, the Painted Desert is no wasteland.

Two life zones, Desertscrub and Desert Grassland, dominate the Painted Desert, providing habitats for hundreds of birds, reptiles, amphibians, and mammals. The golden eagle, horned lark, sage sparrow, raven, canyon wren, and yellow-billed cuckoo are among the 48 resident and 125 migrato-ry birds that are at home in the Petrified Forest and Painted Desert. A partial catalogue of other crea-tures includes short-horned and collared lizards, bull snake, western rattlesnake, mule deer, prong-horn, prairie dog, black-tailed jackrabbit, porcu-pine, kit fox, coyote, badger, bobcat, and raccoon.

Someone once asked me the best time of year to visit the Petrified Forest and Painted Desert. As I pondered the question, I thought of the time when I passed through the sun-drenched landscape after a winter storm to see multicolored mudstone cones capped with snow; or the windy day in spring when I stood beside Grand Falls on the Little Colorado and watched millions of cubic feet of silt-laden chocolate water plunge over the cataract and thought, "There goes the Painted Desert"; or the time in August after the Navajo-named "male rains" of a lightning-punctuated summer thunderstorm had dumped almost an inch of water on the parched ground and the desert was suddenly green. "Anytime," I answered. "Come anytime."

◆ **Petrified Forest National Park**
P.O. Box 2217
Petrified Forest, AZ 86028
602-524-6228

METEOR CRATER

PETER KRESAN

Meteor Crater lies about 10 miles south of Milepost 233 off Interstate 40, 35 miles east of Flagstaff. It's well worth a stop.

Lots of meteorite craters pock the earth's surface. But Meteor Crater is far and away the best preserved of these and the first to be recognized as having been caused by a meteor impact.

About 23,000 years ago a fiery ball of almost pure iron, 80 to 100 feet in diameter, plunged through the atmosphere and crashed at a velocity of 43,000 miles per hour. Weighing some 63,000 tons, it dis-placed 300 million tons of rock to create a crater 594 feet deep, and almost 1 mile across.

Because of its resemblance to craters on the Moon's surface, Meteor Crater was used as a training ground for Apollo astronauts. Among the features at the Meteor Crater Museum are displays on the Apollo pro-gram, lunar geology, and the Voyager mis-sions. Movies on the crater's history and space exploration are also shown.

Viewing tubes mounted on an observation deck overlooking the crater's rim spot thrust faults, a dry lake bed, drill holes, a tunnel where drilling tools were repaired, and other features.

INDIAN COUNTRY TRAVEL

◆ ◆ ◆ ◆ ◆

◆ROAD CONDITIONS: All U.S. highways, state roads, and main tribal roads are paved. Secondary roads are usually graded and graveled. However, travel off recognized and numbered roads is strongly discouraged. Inquire locally about road conditions.

◆SERVICE: Keep your gas tank full, and be sure to check fluid levels. It can be a very long way between service stations.

◆WEATHER: Be prepared for anything. Winters, in recent memory, have had snows 6 and 7 feet deep. Summer temperatures are often over 100 degrees. Winds may blow with gale force any time of the year. High-profile vehicles may have to find a place out of the wind and stop. Tune in to radio weather information.

◆FLASH FLOODING: After hard rains, normally dry washes often become roaring streams from storms that are miles away. Never attempt to cross a running creek.

◆DUST STORMS: Some areas (usually marked with warning signs) are prone to dust storms. If caught in a dust storm, try to find a place to get off the road. Turn off your headlights (someone following you might think you're on the road and run into the back of your vehicle). Be patient. Dust storms are usually brief.

RANDY PRENTICE

◆ANIMALS: Much of Indian Country is open range as pictured above. Cattle, horses, sheep, and goats often graze the roadside. Flocks of sheep accompanied by shepherds and dogs are commonly seen crossing roads. Night driving requires special attention. Dark colored cows and horses are very hard to see. If all you see is two shining dots, it is probably the animal's eyes.

◆WATER: Always carry extra drinking water (and food) in your vehicle in case of a breakdown.

◆SPEED LIMITS: Obey them. Speed limits, stop signs, and all other regulations are strictly enforced by tribal police.

(BACK COVER) *In October every leaf is a flower at White House Ruin in Canyon de Chelly National Monument.*
DICK DIETRICH